T0196321

BASE

You've built the foundation of who you are by the age of six

TAMARA LEIGH

authorHOUSE®

AuthorHouse™
1663 Liberty Drive
Bloomington, IN 47403
www.authorhouse.com
Phone: 1 (800) 839-8640

Published by AuthorHouse   02/15/2017

ISBN: 978-1-5246-7101-3 (sc)
ISBN: 9781-5246-7100-6 (e)

BASE

BY: TAMARA LEIGH

ABOUT THE AUTHOR:

Tamara Leigh is a 37 year old single mother to a beautiful little girl, Me'Arah Izabel Ennis. Tamara was born and raised in Boston, Massachusetts.

Ever since she was a little girl she loved to write, at an early age she had such a creative mind, writing her first play at the age of eight. She went from writing stories, to writing music, to writing poetry on a local level.

"Writing is just my gift from God", she would say.

My Daddy would always tell me that I love too hard, but the truth is, I believe that's what gave me the ability to make words have so much emotion. I'm an emotional being. Every time I went through something my father would say, "Just write".

I actually sat down several times to write a book but it never quite felt like it was what I really wanted to say to the world and I would quickly dispose of it. It wasn't until I found this recipe for storytelling and poetry that once finished gave me butterflies. Instantly I knew this was my story.

My life has been an amazing journey that has very high highs and very low lows and I'm excited to share it, with the hopes that it might make someone else feel as though they're not alone or even help change their life.

BASE is the first book of my poetry collection. This is nothing compared to my teenage years my twenties, my thirties and I'm sure that the future holds so much more.

Trust me; I'm just getting started....

YOU'VE BUILT THE FOUNDATION OF WHO YOU ARE BY THE AGE OF SIX

BASE

BY: TAMARA LEIGH

BASE

BOOK 1 OF A COLLECTION

By: Tamara Leigh

YOU'VE BUILT THE FOUNDATION OF WHO YOU ARE BY THE AGE OF SIX

I dedicate this book to my parents,
Linda and Albert Montgomery
This was a hard read for them and I had no
intentions of my truths being their pain
You are the best parents in the world
Without you I would not be the incredible woman I am today
We are all perfectly imperfect
In fact the only thing perfect is love

I love you!
Tamara Leigh

I'm from a generation that had already overcome the division of religion, Christopher Columbus, the slaughter of Native Americans, smallpox, slavery, women gaining the right to vote, segregation, Ku Klux Klan, the Great Depression, polio, Black Panthers, Baby Boomers, Woodstock, Robert Kennedy Jr. and Martin Luther King Jr's assassination, the first person walking on the moon, cocaine, crack cocaine, hip hop, open displays of homosexuality, AIDS, the first black president, and now global warming......

AMERICA

They say it's the home of the free and the land of the brave

Stolen, infected

Built by slaves

You can be anything

The devil himself

Gain superstardom, political, systematic wealth

Fear nothing at all but fear itself

If you can't be you

Be somebody else

Full of opportunity

The limits the sky

So come get your piece

Of this American pie

See, I come from a mixed background, however I identify as a black woman with light skin thick lips and soul. I've experienced every part of America's history in so many different ways. Through generations of passed on transgression that not only left imprints on who I am, but also pulled me further and further away from the perfect person God had created me to be.

They say it's hard for a black man, but at
least he has the love of a black woman

A Woman's Life

Life is nothing more than a series of events that
leave imprints from the past on the future

From lessons we've learned as children, to the lessons we teach our own

It is a cycle of energy transferred

The point isn't to be right

It's to be present

To be heard

And even more so, to be felt

We learn the most in times of struggle

We love the most in times of despair

For anything complete has reached its end

As women we breathe life, our hands are healing
and our love balances the world

As women we are selfless, our words sacred, our prayers
stretch far into the heavens raining down on the earth

And when our work is done our lessons are immeasurable,
forever praised and respected like the most high

Life is nothing more than a series of events that
leave imprints from the past on the future

A cycle of energy transferred

Summers are what I remember best. The mind has a funny way of retaining information. Sometimes you don't even know all the information you have stored in your thoughts. Some things resurface simply from a smell or a sound and can become so alive that you feel yourself in that very moment.

I was a Daddy's girl.....

Activist

He was a voice with a message

A speaker

Like preachers, politicians or activist

He came from a generation of:

Afros

Black fist

Platforms

And hair picks

He was hard to depict because of his mix

Bronze skin: German, Black and Cape Verdean

He smelled of hardwood and incense

The flavor of hidden innocence

What a cool cat

Draped in colorful cottons and crowned with a tilted top hat

Like a fresh glass of water

Drove a Duce and a quarter

I fell in love once he called me his daughter

I called him Dad

Some called him Jazz

Others called him Money, Goldie or Cash

A few called him fast

The ladies called him Honey

But there was nothing about the man that you couldn't take from me

Because I wear his skin, his feet and his eyes

His style, his passion and thin body size

I walk with pride to the sound of piano keys

And live my life like an old school beat

POWER

My father's family is the most diverse which meant his family was more affected by the American dream. His mother Isabel Devega was born in Providence, RI. Her parents were natives of Brava, Cape Verde making her of African and Portuguese descent, bred from an island that was designed for the transatlantic slave trade and victims of religious persecution. They would move to America, raise children and settle. My father's mother would grow to bear children with James Montgomery, a German mulatto man of Cambridge, MA. What a beautiful mix, creating strong featured children with light skin, curly hair and sharp African features.

<u>Who</u>

Hide your tongue and hold your head up

Just fit in

City lights and opportunity

We've come so far and this revolving door keeps turning

So as long as I can smile who cares if I'm empty?

I carried my children from huts to high rises

From cachupa to cordon bleu

So smile because these opportunities only come once in a life time

Paint your nails, press your clothes and get ready to dance

You're beautiful

Hide those scars and take what's yours

I travelled overseas and left my culture at the docks

It's nothing to walk away

I just want to be free

America is baked in ovens

Mystery movies and silence

And it's time

To

Eat

My mother was born in Birmingham, Alabama to Tomali Dye and Thomas Devine Davis. Though segregation had a great impact on her upbringing, the loss of her heritage from slavery had destroyed anything further to clearly reference her true identity. I guess this was the gift and the curse. On one hand it allowed her to only know vague stories of the destruction of her ancestors so the reality had less of an affect on her behavior. Especially by 1949 the year in which she was born. There was still this underlying understanding that America was built from the blood of her greats, and the fact that signs directing colored people to back doors and banning them from some locations made the unseen bondage and abuse of her people closer than the 84 years of freedom that had past. The gift was that she arose from a time of great power, leadership, unity and, oh yes, music. All of those things made that American dream seem all so real. She was 10 years old when Motown first hit the ground running imagine the possibility that could make someone feel.

She was a real southern peach, very kind hearted and giving. Her family would eventually uproot and relocate to Boston, MA where segregation wasn't so blunt. It had a subtle undertone that made you feel more confused than rejected.

JOY

Red bones and bounce

Bright smiles and hot combs

Biscuits and collard greens

Sequence

Sweet love that dripped with peach flavor

Shiny brown skin

White teeth

Small waist and long legs

That twist

Rhythm in your stride

Pride

Fried green tomatoes, white rice and peas

Vaseline and hair grease

Fish fries

Card games

And whisky

Family reunions

Martin Luther King

Soul trains

Gold chains and hoops

Daisy dukes

Tie dye

Turtlenecks and go-go boots

Baptized in Baptist congregations

Fans and breath mints

Tight curls and pigtails

Decorations and party lights

Sewing needles

Road Trips and catalogs
Yes ma am's, thank yous and brunch
No back talk
Behind your back talk
Hush
And bless your food

SECRETS

My parents chased the American dream, so I spent many days at Nanny's house. Nanny was my Great Aunt. My mother was the only one of my grandmothers' children welcomed in Nanny's house. The others weren't "wholesome" enough, I guess. I had a special bond with Nanny's only daughter; she was my God mother and one of my mother's closest friends. I called her Aunt Jean, it was strange because she would never let other people see how close we were, we connected only in private and everyone else just thought she was mean.

Nanny's house was full of dos and don'ts, good and bad, right and wrong, but I learned it's the things we hate the most that tear us apart. I think it was crack cocaine that brought the devil to Nanny's door, but I had my own devils looking to tear me down. I was often teased by my two older cousins that spent their days there as well. I'm not sure if it was because I was born the first light skin girl in our generation or if they were just mean, but the treatment would follow me as I grew older and they would always try to tear me down.

In a world of good and bad there were always degrees of separation, but what made us different?

It shows

Trick

Or

Treat

You'll never know - Loving enemies

They say we are the same

But you don't look like me

Hidden toys

Mockery

I'd only lead you astray

So bring all your treasures along with you

When you come outside to play

I can see we're different but they say we are the same...

You look just like your Daddy

Yea, he's the one to blame

Every time you come around our attitudes will change

When we're alone I'll open up smiling in your face

But we just want your stories to tear apart your name

We'll never encourage greatness because we are not the same

GAME

My dad was a "ladies man" and enjoyed the freedom of life; I enjoyed just being in his presence. I wouldn't talk much. I just watched how he did things and listened very closely to his music. He always played some form of jazz, groove, or soul music. He didn't really have a big family like my mother. Although I knew his siblings and mother, it wasn't the same kind of bond that my mother's family had. They kept to themselves and focused more on their own issues than everyone else's. He had a **BUNCH** of friends that he spent his time with, and they became his family.

Ties

Like You

You warm me with heat

Colors like

Pink, baby blue and yellow

Mixed up and so soft

Like

A light saxophone playing in low key

Smooth

Like

A jazz beat

I'd say the wind is the bass

And

OH how it surrounds me

I can hear the trees shake

They sound like

Tambourines

And the birds

The birds would be like

Strings

The rhythm of your mind makes the eyes see the earth sing

Like

Baby lets cruise away from here

Like

Loving you is easy 'cause you're beautiful

Like

I just wanna see my lovely sunshine

Like

If loving you is wrong I don't wanna be right

Or like

Unforgettable in every way

Melodies playing in the city streets with no speakers

Just the sound of the earth

The sound of a heart

The sound of a stare

The sound of a child

The sound of a woman

The sound of a man

The sound of love

**From then on I looked for the sound
of him in every male I met...**

My dad took his time to make sure everything was a lesson. Telling me the safest way to enter the house, what he thought about my friends, how to save money, and even how to care for plants. He had his own florist business on the side and often took my brother and myself on jobs. He had contracts with a number of banks and businesses in the Boston area. His business was called **Life of Plants.** We were responsible for spraying down the leaves and picking up the dead ones. He'd even have us pedal flowers on the corner of our street for holidays. We learned how to make flower arrangements, communicate our own sales and handle money; we actually got paid for that work.

My Dad would always carry a gun. He made sure we saw it and fully understood its purpose.

EXERCISE

Preparation

I want my lessons engraved on your mind like forms of habit

Pay attention

I need the satisfaction of knowing that I'm present even when I'm absent

Listen

I can read your body's disposition and know exactly how you're feeling

Stand up

I'll tell you everything you need to know about
the world because I believe it's yours

Grab it

From art strokes to designer clothes

From vineyards to country roads

Tree swings to dancing

From democrat to republican

Working to hustling

Education to gentrification

I know it all

Tough love

Nothing comes easy

Grind

Who needs hugs and kisses

Dreams and wishes

When you have

Blood, sweat and tears

Suck it up

It took years

To get right here

So enjoy the view

But you won't forget the struggle

Work

My mother was the exact opposite of my father. Her house was disorganized and always had different people frequenting on a regular bases. Everyone in our family lived there at one point or another. I was a teenager by the time I finally got my own room. It was loud and always had something going on. My mother would work most of the time and left her younger siblings to watch over us, or she sent us to Nanny's house around the corner.

You can't open your door for everyone

**Sometimes you have to meet them in
the alley that they came from**

Poison

How do you get to the soul?

Covered in flesh and deeper than the universe

Valleys low are most travelled because the eyes lead to the heart

But how do you get to the soul?

Unwrapped like presents

Even untouched by Gods

Only snakes would stoop so low

Spread wide between thighs

In dark lights

And

Bed sheets

Uncovered like graves resting in peace

Not created in the womb

More like flowers making pollen for honey walls

Sweet fruit forbidden in sacred parks

Like touching the sun

Hot

Full of passion, secretions and life

How could you take a soul?

LOST AND...

BROKEN

It was easy for me to let the pain creep in and overpower everything
The pain could keep me still in the shadows of my thoughts
Wondering if anything was worth It
In a world so big yet so empty It was deeper to
travel through the depths of my mind
I could cross seas and find curse to things that were broken
Yet I was so broken
From the reality that stole my heart
Was it this ghetto that brought me so much pain?
The fact that I had come from a place where everything was broken
Where my sexuality meant more than my dreams
It was the only thing that most people could see
Pretty hurts
Like a centerpiece of flowers all for the people to see
How beautiful to watch them die
Quenching its thirst from small offerings
Torn from its roots, ripped from the ground
Delighted they watched
I could sit in this pain for eternity gathering
broken pieces of a perfect life
Putting them together to create temporary
happiness that could only live in a spotlight
Fed from the validation of mainstream thinking that
labeled everything from behavior to thought
from product to production
And I was just one more piece outside of the captivity of my mind
At least there I could travel a thousand times without being
held to a standard that fit the definition of "normal"
I could be nude without temptation
Comfortable in my flesh
I could yell without aggression and still be feminine
I could cry without something being wrong

21

FUCK the labels
I could choose to be weak and strong
Now I'm less than, awkward, I'm placed in a box
That's why it's easier to be pained in my thoughts.

Tough

I often wore my big brother's "hand me downs". My brother was six years older than me so we hardly interacted with one another. When I needed a babysitter he was free to stay with friends and off doing his own thing. We never really got that close I just watched him and he usually complained and kicked me out of whatever he was doing with his friends.

I was on the road of becoming a tomboy. Back then the community helped raise the children. You knew the people on your street and interacted with all the kids in the area. My older brother was now turning into a teenager and I watched as he adapted to the trends and culture of our community.

What don't kill you will only make you stronger

80's Baby

Respectfully tough

Leather

Things came together

Pieces

Fleeces, running suits, and bamboos

Gucci Links

Push-ups and basketball

Run-DMC, EPMD

Kool Moe Dee, Biz Markie

Fresh

Gangsta

High top fades

And natural beauty

Colorful fashion

Drug deals and fast cash

Kangols and boomboxes

Criminal Minded

Block parties and sirens

Mafia, riots, racially driven violence

Cosby show, black recognition

Oprah Winfrey hits television

MONEY

POWER

RESPECT

My mother placed me and my older brother in the METCO program which is a bussing system designed to transport inner city kids into suburban areas in order to make suburban schools more diverse. They were great schools, way better than the low budget Boston Public schools that were in my community. However, there was always a sense of dissimilarity in my schooling. It wasn't the same type that I had received from my family, it was completely different. Not only looks but behaviors were different. There was no struggle, no hustle, and no style; Just black and white.

And here I am reaching six years old

**YOU'VE BUILT THE FOUNDATION OF
WHO YOU ARE BY THE AGE OF SIX**

My Mother, Father, brother and I

Climbing to the top with our Dad

My beautiful Mother

Thank you!

Upon finishing this book I had no idea what to do next. I wondered how the world would receive me and if there was a place for my work in the hearts of others.

If you are reading this then I am one step closer to creating my dream and I thank you!

The biggest lesson I've learned in this process is that the world moves in so many different directions. We can all be in the same place, experiencing the same events and walk away touched in different ways.

I look forward to sharing more of me with you as I am currently working on the next portion of this story: **YOUNG**

Without your support my work is nothing more than what someone doodles on a piece of paper while talking on the phone, temporary and discarded. I hope these words can resonate in your heart as you journey through life and help you to feel some sort of connection with me; For we are all one, set forth to fulfill the same dreams in different places.

I would like to thank everyone I mentioned in this book. My parents for creating me and loving me unconditionally, you are my best friends. My Grandma Tommie for showing me what a woman is made of: Beauty, Grace, Talent and a little bit of Fire. To my Nanna Isabel for showing me how to sit still with myself. My Great Aunt Nanny for teaching me order and showing me how to standup for what I believe in. To my older brother Albie for teaching me to put myself first. Without each of you, I fail to exist. I love you!

Blessings and love,

Tamara Leigh

Tamara Leigh

Printed in the United States
By Bookmasters